CHANCE BODIES

CHANCE BODIES

Donald Illich

THE HILARY THAM CAPITAL COLLECTION
2018 Selections by Joan Larkin

THE WORD WORKS
WASHINGTON, D.C.

THE WORD WORKS
P.O. Box 42164
Washington, D.C. 20015
editor@wordworksbooks.org

Cover art: Janice Cornstalk
Cover design: Susan Pearce Design
Author photograph: Mei Mei Chang

ISBN: 978-1-944585-21-1
LCCN: 2018931394

Acknowledgments

I am grateful to the editors of the publications in which the following poems first appeared or are forthcoming:

Barnaby Jones: "Walking the Suburbs"
The Bakery: "I Want the Medicine"
Barrelhouse: "The Mice Run"
Bird's Thumb: "Theater"
Bluestem: "Islands"
Boog City: "The Labors"
Coconut: "Ghost Immunities"
Cold Mountain Review: "Quiet, Please"
Columbia Online: "Seeing the Average," "Fearsome," "Witnesses,"
        and "Break into the Body"
Cream City Review: "Return My Arms"
Cross Connect Magazine: "Bears Killing Hunters"
Everyday Genius: "Moon Poem"
Folio: "The Park Rangers"
Gargoyle: "Falling"
Gravel: "Worsening the Situation"
Hobble Creek Review: "Wings"
In Posse Review: "Achilles"
Iowa Review: "Sketch of an Astronaut"
JMWW: "Rocket Children"
Leveler: "Dirt Bikes"
Lily: "Secrets of the Underwear Drawer"
LIT: "Bears"
Lullwater Review: "Balloon Animals"
The Bedside Guide to No Tell Motel: "Another Foothold"
Origins Journal: "Smoke"
Phantom Drift: "In the Soda Factory"
Plainsongs: "Kafka the Friendly Ghost"
Rattle: "The Escape Artists"
Kill Author and *Really System:* "Because an Island Is Encouragement"
Sierra Nevada Review: "Dancing with the Snake"

Sixth Finch: "Neighborhood"
Souvenir Lit: "Intercepted by Fire"
Starfish Poetry: "Reversal of Clowns"
The Sulphur River Literary Review: "Enemies"
Topology Magazine: "Propellers"
Verdad: "The Collapse"
VQR Instagram Poem: "You Blackboard"

Some of these poems appeared in a self-published
chapbook, *Rocket Children*.

Thank you to my fellow D.C. poets, especially the Federal
Poets, for their help with my poems, as well as some
Facebook poetry group members, such as Steve Mueske,
Ash Bowen, Hannah Craig, and Bill Neumire. Thanks to my
teachers, Sandra Beasley, Gerry LaFemina, Bruce Snider,
Dana Roeser, Ryan Van Cleave, Mark Cugini, Abdul Ali,
Judith McCombs, and others. Especially, thank you to my
parents, my brothers, and my wife Julia, who makes it all
possible.

for my brother Robb

"Thus all things are but altered, nothing dies."

—Ovid, *Metamorphoses*, Book XV (trans. John Dryden)

Contents

Humans

Sketch of an Astronaut

A man in a spacesuit can go far in this little town,
shaped for farmers, and teens with buckets of turnips
who throw them off trucks at crowds of children.

He has his own source of oxygen, so the smoke
of Cuban cigars at the lodge or the gray clouds
over the daily book burnings don't tear up his eyes
or roll him over into a waiting line of coffins.

Making so much of his big leaps at hopscotch,
he plants flags in housewives' petunias and plays
golf among the asphalt potholes, disappointed
the ball skips across lawns and fails to soar.

When he chaperones the prom with our youngest teacher
he buzzes his words through a white helmet,
dwarfs her hands with his insulated gloves, and
doesn't feel the hot pink lipstick through his visor.

The neighbors find his boot prints, large steps
for a man, at two in the morning outside their launch
pads, where the astronaut creates explosive sounds
with his mouth inside space cars that won't fire.

Before he leaves he sits in a chair at the ladies'
auxiliary, who a week ago drew their first naked man.
No matter how much they plead, the suit stays on.
Around his massive head, they sketch the stars.

Secret Club

Have I joined? Its members don't tell me.
A card might lurk inside my wallet.
A secret handshake may already be part
of my silent vocabulary. Are the fliers
hanging off my doorknobs signs that gates
have been opened, mysteries revealed?

People around me mind their own business,
but what is it, what are they doing?
Fathers throw footballs in exact parabolas.
Uncles take perfect short-cuts to stadiums.
Do they know what's being arranged
in their absence from underground rooms,
clones dressed in scarlet robes twirling
like majorettes in a blood-drinking band?

I'm part of something, but no one wants
me to be sure. They blindfold me,
walk me down earthen steps. All I hear
is the scuffling of clumsy feet, like
trick-or-treaters running for candy.
What do I expect? An explanation
owed the world, a reason for exclusion
from the workings of the universe.

They guide my hand in a circle,
points starting and ending with me:
nothing inside, nothing out, nothing.

Another Foothold

This is a dream.
I'm scaling a cliff
I'd never try in my life.
I've imagined
being atop skyscrapers
or hang-gliding
over the sea,
but I've always fallen,
landed,
then dropped again.

My guide tells me
another safe foothold
is one length away,
but it may as well be miles.
My shoe's a baby rattle,
it shakes over the canyon
and its swooping vultures.

I know how
this trip will end:
a place to step breaks
under my weight,
my hands scratch
at walls that won't
slow me down.
I'm an inverse of sky,
a dark field
of human-shaped stars,
each one crashing
without a last wish.

Hitting the peak,
I spot you below,
feeding whispers to deer,
yelling at hungry bears
to behave.

It's too far down
for you to hear me.
I want to shout,
I'm all right,
I don't need you.

My lungs
don't give me enough
air to speak—
you're fading into woods,
part of a lush fern,
a sprig of wild berries,
beautiful things
I can't see from here.

To Beatrice

When I was young we had to walk
six miles through Hades to get to school.

We didn't have protection from Satan's minions, either.
If a demon ripped apart a fellow student,
we cinched our backpacks, kept tromping toward class,
knowing post-traumatic stress didn't excuse lateness.

I can't tell you how many wounds and burns
I received, or how difficult it was to ignore
the screams and torments of the damned,
who bothered us for news of the world.

After school, though, Mom washed off the soot,
handed me a nice cup of hot cocoa
with miniature marshmallows. I'd go upstairs
to write to my pen pal overseas.

In her photo she smiled angelically
next to two cherubs who guided her
through puffy clouds and pearly gates,
to enter the building where she drilled verbs
to learn my language.

Even if I had to run through hellfire,
I knew one day I'd come to visit her.

Ghost Immunities

The "deep mystery" of melted steel.
Here comes a rain cloud. Water beats fire.

These were years of billowing smoke.
The torch will make the flame design flicker.

And the secret of steel, used to fire
a home barbecue. Smelting iron ore.

Years of great mystery: Will dad find another
job soon? Are we poor now? The main exit

near the fire was blocked. A source of
conflict in the city. The alarm goes off

in the middle of the night. The many
immunities Ghost has covered up are

contained under pressure in a cylinder.
Wishful thinking. Middle shift and layoffs.

December Song

Turn the star, let its light dazzle
someone else. Throw the tree in a heap,
with the after-Christmas blues
dangling from its branches. There's no
manger where a baby waits expectantly
for a gift of cologne and a wallet.
The animals do not sing or bow down,
the wise men laugh as they get lost.
All that's on the horizon is time
burning the desert, rivers, hills,
shoving everything into its deep mouth
like the sweetest dessert eternity
ever knew. Carry the cross away
in your hands, snort the frankincense,
dab the myrrh on your skin. Look
at the falls where the calendar breaks
into new months, into centuries
not yet imagined. The star spins overhead,
but it's unreachable. The big gold ball
drops, and we're all frozen in flashes.

Farm

i am the farm chickens
pigs cows goats horses
i am the pond filled
with fish the barn covered
in hay the tractor gnawing
grass i am the clear sky
mirrored in puddles i am
the farmer dressed in denim
i am his straw hat shielding
sun i am his suspenders keeping
up his pants i am the boy
playing with sticks i am
the wife frying eggs i am
the gravestone at the edge
of the property i am the ghost
that moans at night i am
the stars that suddenly appear
i am the light that is life
i am the dark that hides it
i am growing inside her
i am quaking in him i am
the hospital i am the bed
i am the kid visiting the stone
i am the words he says
i am the way he bends down

Walking the Suburbs

There are no sidewalks. Striped hoses snake out
to trip you. The faucet's mouth is clean and
guiltless. Children enter SUVs, exit teenagers

drinking for the weekend. You kick their bottles
over park soccer goals. You examine their gum
wrappers for pain and lipstick. You hide ripped

progress reports in your pockets. The old hate
the heat. Men who live alone set up kid traps in
their backyards. A bear wanders in from the woods,

trailed by a news crew. It refuses to jump on a
trampoline or eat people. The *Keep Off* signs are
too flimsy to support you. Tree houses are out

of reach, guarded by security dads' vigilant eyes.
Cars spray alarms in your face if you sit on their hoods.
A fish on the back windshield means they own guns.

At the last court you see a mud puddle, where a
turtle paddles around. It could climb over cracks
in the asphalt, it's big enough. It prefers to live

in filth, bottle caps floating by its black shell.
You jump inside its crater; dirty water splashes you.
You're stuck on your back, you can't turn over.

Propellers

We never traveled over bridges.
It was too dark under their skin.
The monsters wanted to attack.

Instead, we floated in airplanes,
propellers spinning like our hearts,
as we counted clouds under us.

When we reached our destination,
we planted a flower for our birth
in this soil, as if we were brand new.

The natives would greet us
with burgers and fries, foreign
to our world, as well as taxis.

We remembered how we walked
everywhere, chewed on carrots.
Our blood rejected this alien food.

We'd be told to sleep in a bed.
We felt nostalgia for hanging off
the ceiling, how we usually slept.

But soon the bats would return,
our dream friends, and we'd sweep
our world for insects and fruit.

There were no skyscrapers,
or monuments to anyone dead.
Everything stood for the living.

Neighborhood

When I arrived everyone was happy to see me.
They welcomed me to burning barbecues,
threw me in a pool as a lark. I could've drowned,
but I didn't blame them. If anything, I should've
expected jokes, like how they removed families'
houses, leaving pits of mud and pipes in their place.
Or how they set leaves on fire with gas and propane,
so they would resist extinguishers. Still, everyone
had smiles on their faces, did jumping jacks at 6 a.m.,
sold their junk to each other on yard sale weekends.
When a child went missing they never worried,
though bears grumbled close by, no one covered
the wells. I learned how to laugh at funerals,
how to reassure myself that I was still breathing.
Nothing would happen to me that I hadn't earned
by being born. Roses died, milk soured on doorsteps.
I lay on graves: my first one, and the second to come.

The Train Fall

Passengers dropped to the ground,
imagining they had parachutes when
they hit the rocks. Cars on fire

were candles on a steel birthday cake.
No one was there yet to blow them out.
The luggage added fuel to the flames,

which rose higher with each bite
they took of the train. Around it
mountains added darkness to light,

shuddering from explosions. Ghosts
floated upward, toward a melting sky.
They talked to one another about life.

They didn't yet know what death was.
Instead, they recalled a touch football
game at Thanksgiving, a hot fudge sundae

after school. They wanted to hold on tight
to those memories, as stars revealed
their lights, pushing gold pins in felt,

so they could be removed by the moon,
a pasted-on satellite, the only thing
left with the eyes and grin to be alive.

In the Soda Factory

At first it is a gray building
lit up with rainbow lights,
the name of its brand
stained red on its walls.
I know I have to go there
to help the factory run,
because the clear bottles
have not been filling up,
there's a part or a lever
that is not operating.
When I climb toward the top,
I realize it's really a stadium,
and monks have taken
each seat, standing up,
chanting their sacred songs.
I wonder why I don't have
a robe, why I'm dressed
in blue jeans and a t-shirt.
Below us the football teams
prepare to kick off, cameras
showing every movement,
each tackle and pass clearly.
I don't believe in anything,
so I'm afraid the brothers
will find out, that they'll
punish me with a hair-shirt,
or lock me in a dark room.
I realize the scoreboard
shows the number of bottles
that are being broken,
that I am failing my job.
It doesn't matter how hard
I try, I cannot find where

the machinery is located.
I run up and down the floors,
wishing I had a heavy cross
dangling from my neck, a way
to show God I understood,
that I should be filled with him,
if I were to be carbonated
with the black liquid, bubbled
enough to reach the clouds.

Because an Island Is Encouragement

How able am I to sail across this sea?
My boat leaks. The sun melts the deck.
Wind won't show to blow me forward.
Water won't slide me to the island

no matter how many TVs, blenders,
and stereos I throw into its maw.
When I get there I'll burn my clothes.
I'll dance around without a three-piece suit.

If there's an office I'll shut its doors.
No need for work when pineapples
dive-bomb my mouth. No microwaves
when I can cook my food on a rock.

If only this ship would take off!
I wouldn't have to look at this reflection
of the grave I've been digging. Yellow
folders as my bones. A desk as my skull.

Witnesses

The difficulty is we were able to see,
to point our eyeballs at the problem,
feel its colors massing on our vision.
If we hadn't been able to watch it,
we would've slept at night, crawling
into covers like a banana peel, waiting
for the big mouth of unconsciousness
to envelop us. Being witnesses hurt
our bodies, left bruises on our faces.
We weren't the types that wanted to know
what evil was, what bushes it hid in,
what tombs darkness could erupt from.
Instead, we'd rather stare into the sun,
let blindness see everything as beauty,
one solid ray of gold that stunned us.
We'd stumble from street to building,
from floor to bedroom, believing all
was as it had been, when the talons
clutch on to our legs, bats fly over
our heads, fluttering hair, leading us
into caves we can't come back from.

In Which Everything Becomes Morning

The alarm clock is morning.

It rings each second,
intensely warning me
of the sun.

The bed is morning.
I start the day there,
slingshot into waking
from dreams.

The chair is morning.
The computer is morning.

I sit to check weather forecasts,
tap my keyboard to discover
whether there will be rain.

The stairs are morning.
The pills are morning.
The yogurt is morning.

How I get down one step
after another, swallowing
the sky's orange, filling up
with blue radiance in my bowl.

The clothes are morning.
The shoes are morning.
The open door is morning.
The kiss is morning.

I wear what I can to be glorious.
I turn the doorknob to the outdoors.
I take clear footsteps in the mist,
cumulus above me, shining.

Our eyes are morning.
Our hands are morning.

Break into the Body

Force the limbs to fall under the Christmas
wreath. To touch the nose, wondering
when it will turn red. Make it flee
from fireworks in the yard, then touch
the charred remains. Force it to run
through waves bashing against a beach,
so the body can remember what it was like
to excuse yourself from the sea. When spring
arrives, let the limbs renew like bushes
and leaves, the sprouting of green from ice.
The cherry blossoms will return soon,
and this time the hands won't break them,
leaving them for others to enjoy. In summer
the heat will overcome flesh and blood.
They'll lie on the towel, sweating,
sand encrusting the legs. Eventually,
there will be no season and no love.
The corpse will become a time machine
that sets itself on fire, that quietly stops
as smoke rises from its face and arms.

The Labors

I was prepared to meet my obligations.
To salt a lake until it was ready
to boil eggs. Send a satellite
into subversive orbit. Run a kissing
bandit ring, stealing lips in the darkness.
Except I broke my skeleton
when I missed the sky.
I stumbled around, my skull cracked
in half, nerves on fire. The authorities
told me I had no excuse.
They promised to dangle me over a pool
of alligators, which hadn't been fed,
which would like a taste of humanity.
They mentioned a firing squad
that was waiting to fill me full of holes.
So, I pulled my castle of salt to the edge.
I put the rocket on my back,
fired it into the cosmos.
My chapped lips could hardly stand
another face. They stopped threatening me.
They asked me if I'd ever been in love.
No, I said, and I never will.
The sky is prepared
to snap me in half again.

Falling

Some practiced falling from buildings,
arms spread out, nerves jangling,
a song of wonder in their hearts.

They landed OK, concrete cushioning
them. This wasn't like our nightmares,
when they broke apart like cheap toys.

Their strings still pulled happy greetings,
voices sweet, unyielding to disaster.
Others wouldn't leave the ground,

stuck like a pin in the grass. They lived
on the first floor, glaring at everyone
who shot upward in glass elevators.

In their dreams they flew planes
over targets, where they dropped
miles of flame, enough to melt towns.

City Waltz

In the city we tackle each other for crying,
crushing those tears against the sidewalk.
When someone whistles while they work,

we start whistling back, till his melodies
have been drowned out by our noise.
Sometimes we'll let a woman dance by herself,

but we'll observe her carefully, make sure
she's not too joyful in her movements.
If she is, we force her to twist till she drops.

We move through streets and alleys,
stop at bars where we drunkenly smear
everyone with invective. On the way home

we bang trash cans, summoning
the neighborhood to flood out, follow
our lead. Our music is for stoplights

and gang fights, ambulances and sewer
backups. We waltz to it through the night,
bounce ourselves off walls and streetlights.

Transformations

Temporarily Human

We sleep in the closet, hanging upside
down like bats. When we take off from
that spot, we flap our arms, seek out fresh
fruit. Echolocation keeps us from running
into anyone, but people still seem bothered

by our high-pitched screams. At work
we've turned into butterflies. Floating by
co-workers' cubicles, we drive them so mad
they swing at us with nets. Escaping,
we settle at our desks, letting our wings

tap out the memos, hitting number keys
with our antennae. When we've finished
our days, we swoop to elevators as cardinals.
Friends remark on our beauty, but we do not
let it influence us. We'll still devour all

the seed in their bird feeders, sneaking
into their backyards when it's dark. Before
they have a chance to shine lights on us,
we've disappeared into the shadows, ravens
that perch on windows. "Nevermore,"

we caw, "nevermore." Our spouses wake
to shoo us away, but by morning we've
already plunged into our clothes, eating
Grape-Nuts, temporarily human, though we'll
always believe we're creatures that soar.

Darker

You walk to your therapist
through a corporate park.
Buildings glitter with glass.
Stubborn cars still fill
parking lots. Grown trees
carry flocks of blackbirds.
Their wings are dark leaves
that suddenly fall, spin
in the sky with loud squawks,
then resettle the branches.
You think of what you want
to say, but the birds keep
disturbing your concentration.
You imagine flying with them,
miles of winged darkness.
"What does it all mean?"
Above the Earth you don't care.
You are free, frightening.
You dare the evening
to be darker than you.

Chance Bodies

They tried to pull me apart.
One hand on a leg, another
stretching an arm. I could say

nothing, my mouth sewn up,
my eyes plastic discs, painted
black and white. I wished

I was bigger so I could
stop them, smother their faces
with fabric. My hair threads

swayed as they fought
over my body. It was chance
that I existed in this form.

A boy for the vicious,
who could've played with me,
fed me invisible cookies

and tea. I thought about all
the creatures and humans
I could've been. A grizzly

chasing these children, a dog
fetching a chew toy, a parent
catching the kids tearing dolls.

It was not my destiny
to be this way, I swore.
Somewhere in another world

I was delighted by a lover.
I rearranged my arms around
her. I kissed her with real lips.

Return My Arms

You don't understand my attitude.
When my arm started to fall off,
I thought it was normal—
who can say what the body does and why it does it?

Its aversion to work never
stopped it from stapling papers
when my boss stumbled by my door, drunk on PowerPoints.
Its exhaustion never prevented ejaculations from rolling out
like a new line of vacuum cleaners.

Losing my arms when you scampered
out of my forest was to be expected,
a side effect of youth's Viking funeral,
Duran Duran cassettes and jean jackets
burning on the pyre.

You can't stick my shoulders back in
so I can make roast beef sandwiches without sighing,
conduct an orchestra without sobbing on the woodwinds.

I could just go out and play again,
start my childhood over, learn
to admire Dick and Jane instead of cursing
their elementary love, to spell out words
like "responsibility" and "loyalty"
without shooting milk out my nose.

Visit me again and bring my arms.
I'll still hug them like I embraced you,
forgiving everything they made me do.
How you wished for them once,
though the fingers were wayward,
the hands didn't know what they were doing.

Human Self

Don't forget your human self,
my wife yelled as I left home.
It was a good suggestion.
Yesterday I'd been ridden
in a local race because I was
occupying my horse self,
which loved galloping, victory
wreaths. The other week
I had taken over my squirrel
self, and I busily prepared
for winter for hours, gathering
nuts, stuffing them in trees.

Today would be different, though.
I'd live like I was born, like
I had opposable thumbs,
like $E=MC^2$, like the light bulb,
like indoor plumbing. I didn't
become a coyote to run after
other dogs, or hang off branches,
a sleeping sloth.

I drove my car
through a wilderness road,
where animals called to me
from every thicket. I pressed
the gas, fled deeper into the city,
where the parking space
would magically open,
where I breathed in exhaust,
heard the racket of buses,
the sweet noises of human life.

Achilles

The feet have had it up to here
with the ankles insisting on green socks,
when all they want to feel is grass
on a blank white morning,
dirt in a field that's yet to heal.
They wish to stomp hands
that get all the credit for lifting drinks,
and kick the face, so handsome
to the beloved, a welcome mat
she wipes her lips on.

In the end they break, not like hearts,
but like statues' bases cracking on haunted nights
when marble becomes flesh, horsemen galloping
from pedestals to fight stone cannonballers
across town. Tags hang from them,
obstructing their views of the unmoving body.

Why did it take revenge on itself?
the feet ask themselves, now paralyzed.
Before their heels could kill Achilles,
he had left his shield in the tent,
invited enemy swords inside himself.

The Escape Artists

Why were there more than one of us?
Because it was more shocking

when we both exploded from the safe,
unharmed if short of breath,

dressed in sparkling blue uniforms
to signify our amazing natures.

Other times we'd plunge into water
in chains, stay in the icy deep

for several minutes beyond
what we should've been capable of.

When we emerged it was like exiting
the underworld, coming across as fallen

angels who didn't need anything
on this earth, much less the applause

that avalanched over us. They didn't
see the tricks we had developed,

the broken links, hidden keys,
the practice of bending, pulling muscles.

Why would they imagine this hard work
when their life is about not enduring

pain or danger? Sitting at desks
they quit if they feel eye strain

from staring at the computer screen,
would rather drop change

in a vending machine than walk
to the fridge for a carrot or orange.

We suffer so you don't have to,
is what we think. As an example

of near drowning we are the sacrifice
you won't have to make now,

to short-circuit your life with big flashes
of lightning, risks that could suffocate

you if you guess wrong. To us,
the important thing is the process—

the lack of oxygen, choking on water.
This is where we're alive—not

when you salute us, but when we
praise ourselves with deaths you can't see.

Balloon Animals

No matter how hard I tried I could not twist
the pink balloons into dachshunds to nibble
at the lips of the children, or circular hats,
plastic crowns to turn kids into tyrants.

At parties the other clowns jeered,
poured my seltzer out in the bathroom sink,
stole my giant shoes, threw out playing cards
I truly believed contained magic.

Makeup and blood ran down my chin
each time I fought their pranks—
a wicked punch and a run-in with a unicycle
before thirty-two piled into their car and sped away.

At night, though, my floating blobs rose up,
with fireflies inside, through the summer air.
They were UFOs or the northern lights. They
could have been almost anything, and beautiful.

Theater

I stab you with a sword, you swoon to the ground.
You grab me, threatening me. I break into tears.

I go on and on with my speech without interruption.
You curse the gods, stars, fate, that villain, your life.

I return home with bad news, and you start laughing.
You act as if a ghost is directing your every move.

I play a prank on my friends, enemies, the king, Toad.
You dance with an invisible partner, kissing her lips.

I am persuaded to commit murder to achieve power.
You are hanged by the neck for theft, greed, cowardice.

I somehow see the audience, start talking to them.
You don't understand why I am speaking to thin air.

I leap into the crowd, ask them to take me with them.
You call it witchcraft. You can't get off this stage.

I Want the Medicine

With its side effects
of hangnail, flatulence,
goofiness, unexpected
laughter, subpoenas, political
grandstanding, shyness,
potential gruesome death.
I know it will help me
with my erection and my
hairline. I will stop being
pee-shy. I will be able
to say ABCs and mean it.
I will solve mysteries,
and be immune to theft.
My doctor tells me
I have reached a point
where these drugs don't help.
I must jump over fences
or spray my name on them.
I should run a marathon
where I die and rise
from the grave. Or ask
the coffin salesperson
to discount one, how my death
will give rise to others,
as my loved ones swallow
the pills I failed to, as they
giggle to their last places.

The Collapse

O, forehead, I haven't talked about you
enough. Your story of how I collapsed

is beautiful. How the blood screwed up
its directions, giving my mind something

to fail at. On the sidewalk, I bruised
my bones, closed my eyes like blinds.

The ambulance came, everyone feared it
might be too late. But later that day

I did something else—spoke words backwards,
strung together memories in the wrong order.

You were witness to all this, but what
you recall is her kiss dampening your skin.

Enemies

The enemy of my enemy
and I are now dating.
Maybe we're falling in love.

We discuss secret plots,
nets collapsing over prey,
the whole array of capture
and predator devices
used by spies in movies.

Don't be fooled by baby talk,
or the gentle sway of our arms,
holding hands. We can shout orders
to greasy men carrying pistols
to make up for the loss
of their exploded souls.
One blow from us stops hearts,
plants flowers in graveyards.
We cut hate from the world's design
as easily as we sew our affections.

The day will come soon.
We'll be married, and our best man,
whom we kept close, will self-destruct.
Rings will drop onto our fingers
from his unloved puff of dirty smoke.

Secrets of the Underwear Drawer

What keeps me up at night
are thoughts that unbutton
themselves in mental drawers
I slammed shut years ago,
soldered tight, burned neurons.

Did she? And with whom? Why?
Have I really lost track
of love's capital, misplaced
old names of all its villages?

That's the business of commercials,
repeating their catchphrases
throughout my dream life,
overzealous employees even
bosses hate and wish they
could fast-forward into space.

"She'll never forget a diamond."
What if that's all she remembers?

After returning from the moon
in my electric Elvis costume,
I see her at a pawn shop
negotiating affection's value
at pennies per carat.
I slam a giant sardine against
the display window, cracking it.
I let her know I can help
a gambler with the shakes
by tossing a flaming matchbook
with my name on it toward
her strawberry pinwheel eyes.

Getting up from bed, still
not sure if I'm on Earth,
I dial her number, hear
it's been changed.

In my brain something unzips.

Seeing the Average

The leaves aren't so vivid, more mud-colored
than red and orange. The old buildings
are a lusty black and gray, government hovels
for the bureaucrats to run their wheels in.

Rain sometimes adds interest, forming
puddles in sidewalk depressions, streaking
car windows, shocking clouds into movement.
A snowstorm might insert white everywhere,

but shoe prints dirty the beauty. Employees,
in suits and dresses, hold doors for each other,
welcome them to ugly walls being repaired,
a maze for the workers to find their way into.

In windows they see their wished-for escapes.
To the motorcycles, to the vans, where they can
introduce themselves back into the world,
where light and space chime with their hearts.

Dirt Bikes

Trails dissolving and reforming, laced
with pine needles, chipped rocks, holes,
dirt bikes sliding through the obstacles
without a breath left over, the bottom
rising to meet them, a ditch to leap over,
a thorny bush covered with red berries,
the sky sunny enough to blind any eyes,
where accidents result in white casts
on ankles, wrists, legs, hands, arms,
rocket graffiti covering them in hospitals,
or a safe arrival, sweaty and destined,
the excitement jumping off smiling faces,
until each bike is dragged up the hill again,
heavier each time, until evening arrives,
and they must cover themselves in garages,
where spiders lie on webs, cars have dreams
of being smaller, with handlebars, with speed.

Rocket Children

Our babies are learning to be rockets,
drinking fuel in their formula,
transforming cribs into launch pads,
counting down before collapsing for naps.

We're excited about having the first infants
in space, envision them releasing boosters
on their ways to Mars. Some parents
feel we're being too irresponsible.
What about pink and blue blankets,
mobiles and educational toys,
listening to Mozart for bigger brains,
reading to them to improve vocabulary?

Didn't we know our progeny
would end up blown to pieces?
Our neighbors' re-usable space shuttle child
was entering third grade, God willing,
and wasn't that preferable to burning up
as they re-entered the atmosphere?

A cycle of life would lose its wheels
if we let them fly out the Solar System.
We'd be sad when there was no life,
carrying our rattles and baby chairs
to the curbs for pick up by Goodwill.

We refused to listen to doomsayers,
prepared stands for crowds on porches,
rented video cameras to record the event.
Heat shield diapers would protect them.
Our bedroom mission command centers
would check for weather delays.

On the appropriate day we'd wheel
our children into backyards, kiss them,
salute their bravery. They remember
their coordinates. All that's left is
to gasp in awe as they leave the Earth,
pat ourselves on the back for the life
we've delivered to the universe.

They'll discover more than we ever did
on this planet after hundreds of years
surviving, always looking for a way up.

Smoke

The days I was on fire it never rained.
I turned to smoke, spread myself

across the valley. Smothering people,
stinging their eyes, I regretted

what I had become. Soon, I spread
out so far I had disintegrated.

I woke as a boy again, playing with matches.
I struck one after another, seeking

a spark. Each time I could formulate
warmth, a storm charged over

the horizon. I learned how to freeze
to death, watched my skin shine blue.

My breath left my body without
a letter home. Waking the next day,

the sun didn't wait. It corralled me
with flames. It told me to become ashes.

My Dad Is Springtime, I'm Fall

My dad is the reason plants sprout
from real earth. He twirls his hands
and leaves poke out of stems, trees
float in the area with green halos

of growth. Winter doesn't want to leave
but he summons worms, bugs to eat
the snow, light to surround everything.
I walk through his changes, amazed

by flowers climbing walls, people
dropping coats that paddle toward closets.
I undo everything he does. I rip off
the leaves like they're fly wings. Stems

rot in the ground and are covered by red
and orange. The sun can't defend itself
against me as I open up the darkness.
Ice and sleet prepare their appearances,

as if guests on a talk show, excited
to star. My dad and I look at each other.
We can't stand one another's faces.
We turn away, prepared to end, him

in summer, me in winter. We might
return, we might not see one another again.
I will remember the light that blinded me.
He will recall all his works, gone to waste.

Ladder

A good excuse could help me climb
your forgiveness ladder. At the top
I could shout about your sculptor's figure,
how his fingers molded you
so my Tab A and your Tab B
could form "The Lovers."

People would gather to hear about your miracles,
which I didn't believe until my heart
turned to wine. I could drink it
and always be delirious with your love.

What will probably happen is nothing:
a rung breaking, my body falling flat
to the ground in a loser's impression
I can't dig myself out of. You stand
on a cloud without a care,
declaring my photo to be stamped
on every lightning bolt,
that I receive a shock when each one screws up
and destroys a tree.

The oak where I carved our names
has come to life, stalks me through midnight forests,
pulling its roots behind it,
swiping wildlife in its way.

In hiding I imagine how a mortal and a goddess like you
could unite, a reversal of fortune
Ovid would throw down his pen and laugh at.
Where is that excuse? I ask.
Aren't you the storyteller?
He returns to inscribing transformations

of women into stars, men into beasts,
saying only, It's up to you to narrate your own life.
If you mean it, she'll find
a way to bless you.

So I mean it.
I always have,
every step, though I'm balancing fear
on my shoulders, my boots are made of lead.
I won't be knocked off
until I kiss your icon.

My lips will turn to gold—
everything will become gold—
and though I won't be able to eat and drink,
I'll be full of you.

Operational Definitions

A loin is a basket one puts hopes in, though it's often over-turned by the vicissitudes of time and unattractiveness.

A beloved is a wound that never stops oozing. It waits for the Band-Aid of the affectionate to leave for the medicine cabinet so it can turn its motor off.

A waiver is a rebate mailed for the brain that nature gave you when it was drunk and realized it had been wasting its whole life causing leaves to fall and bodies to rot in the sun.

A suicide is a question that's answered in heaven with another damned knock-knock joke.

A washcloth is a danger to young adults when they unclothe their bodies and reveal talking hairs and puppet shows bursting out of their sternums, who put on a Punch and Judy show that would be banned in most states and jurisdictions.

A leech is a tiger that attaches to the neck and pretends it has claws, wishing it could move up the food chain or drain enough love to live.

A lover is a toy that performs arabesques in a ballet by an unknown choreographer. It comes on at the end of the recital, when tin soldiers in the wings remove their rifles and ballerina dolls can no longer stand on one red foot without bleeding stardust, and it seals the lips of the audience in wax so they can no longer speak.

Quiet, Please

When I was born
my parents gave me a book,
So, You're Going to Die.

It had helpful illustrations:
a clown's body covered in flies,
a man stomped into paste and water,
a skinny woman on her deathbed
giving the Grim Reaper a thumb's-up.

The text clearly stated there was
no hope: ghosts a blue figment
of neurons burning out, angels
a button on a lunatic's uniform,
scarier than words could describe,
syllables inadequate as a lover's
coat laid atop an ocean, his beloved
sinking down and passing away.

My parents told me to return
the book to the shelf, play awhile
in the sandy box, the marriage
bed, the grandfather's clock.

I sat all day and read it, dazed
as seconds faded with every letter.

I tried to finish the alphabet,
but Z tapped me on the shoulder,
snatched my library card, hushed
me out the door, saying, "Quiet, please.
People are trying to sleep."

Creatures

Kafka the Friendly Ghost

He spends a lot of time starving himself
of food he won't eat, though he's nice about it.
He says he can turn me into a cockroach to scuttle
along the floor to scare my family, but promises
he'll change me back. He hides from three other
ghosts: one puts him on trial for a crime he didn't
commit; another straps him to a machine that
writes nasty words in his spirit; the last traps him
in a castle where he fills out endless forms
of the afterlife. He's always saved by a smiling
blonde boy who pulls him from the oven, turns
faucets on so he pours out showerheads like gas.

In his spare time, and all of it is spare, he solves
mysteries: Whatever happened to Josephine
the Mouse? Where did the chimney sweep go?
Who wrote a letter to his father and why won't
he read it? None of the cases is ever solved.
He stands at a gate, patiently, cheerfully,
watching other spirits open the door. He's waiting
for a sign from the one who'll let him pass.
If he's there, if he exists, he's waiting, too.

You Blackboard

You blackboard, you darkness wiped clean.
You map to integers, you land of equations.
You place I can deposit all my thoughts
as if they were eggs in a carton, 13 of them.
You dagger into education, you rebellions
jumping up and down, punching at the sun.
You family of resemblances, each sketch
in chalk erased, only to be drawn again,
fiercer, angrier, not believing in anything.
You reason to live longer, the historical facts,
the ways to solve their problems, turn them real.
You flu, virus, cold, disease, cancer, death.
You pledge of allegiance, you cheating scandal.
You teacher's pet, you sprinkler of white dust.

Reversal of Clowns

Putting makeup on the backs of our heads,
we smiled with our necks at the children.
They slipped deep into circus nightmares,
not quite sick enough to die of fright.

We crawled into our Bug car backwards,
drove through the hospital halls in reverse.
As we traveled, the elderly patients grew
younger, jumped out of their wheelchairs,
flung spit wads through our open windows.
The doctors shrank beneath stethoscopes.
Nurses took their dolls' fake temperatures.

We backed out of the building's exits,
pumped ourselves up into human balloons.
The wind changed direction, whipped off
red noses, funny hats, and white gloves.
We expected to keep them, even in the air.

Floating in the gray sky into last week,
we predicted storms that would hit us
whether we liked it or not. Below us,
we saw disasters we could've prevented
if we'd been able to land safely. Children
pointed to us as clouds that had been dyed
by Jesus. Adults, afraid of the unknown,
said we were signs for their new religions,
or a plot by the army across the border
to spy on their soldiers' patterns of defense.

No one laughed at us, not even Neanderthals
who discovered fire when Mittens messed up
a flaming juggling trick. History knows now:
the clown is the Prometheus of us all.

Worsening the Situation

It's bad enough that the grizzlies
roared at us, hardly twenty yards
from our car. I had to roll down

the windows, smear lard on my skin,
and whistle, "Come and get it!"
The family that survived remind me

how I strung a tightrope over
the lion exhibit at the zoo, dressed
as an antelope, smelling like red meat.

How I insulted every mamma
of the Marines at the bar, without
knowing the slightest self-defense.

It would be best if I were restrained
by ropes, chains. That a gag be sealed
over my unfortunate mouth. Always

I escaped whatever prison held me,
throwing off restraints, wiggling through bonds.
It was my duty to worsen the situation.

My brain always had another good idea.
It soon woke to see me in a full body cast.
My limbs suspended. A straw though my lips.

The New Bird

Nobody told me I was a bird.
When I laid an egg they fried it,
finished it off for breakfast
before I could see the proof.

They removed my feathers
while I slept, pushed them deep
into cases to make pillows.
I had dreams about falling,

cliff walls spiraling near me,
but then flapping my arms,
finding myself aloft in the air.
My beak was not a regular mouth,

opening oddly, but they said
I would have to live with it.
One day at a pond I looked
in the water, saw my reflection

and a swan's. We were brothers,
it seemed, and I knew the truth.
My human family would mourn,
but their deception meant

I would never see them again.
In the flock I flew to Canada.
We formed a black V in the sky.
We darkened the earth below us.

The Park Rangers

They love to scatter picnics
with warnings about bears,
then eat what's left:

pickles and honey, whole
submarine sandwiches.
When gathering the animals

they lay down the law:
no more walking upright
when the humans are around,

no more opposable thumbs
(that's what people do, it would
disturb them). The rangers

ride around with heavy metal
blasting, imagine themselves
as conquering warriors.

They ambush neighboring
park stations, plant
stakes at the geyser.

At night before they sleep
they turn off the trees, add
the owl and the moon, subtract

the sunlight and the heat.
In their rooms their helmets
glow with an eerie flame.

Wings

We sleep in the midst of wings. They flutter over our noses making us sneeze. They tickle the insides of our lungs. They mess up our hair and scratch up our legs. We don't call them wings, because we think they're just air. Except the spirits know how to remain invisible, even as they do the work through us that we couldn't do without them.

The Mice Run

If the past is a lady, then mine
is angry with me for some reason.

Maybe I didn't take out a Day
to the curb so it could be trashed

with all the others I can't remember.
Or I got drunk and upset a Month

which turned into December before
my eyes, freezing me out on the patch

of broken down, dangerous Winter.
Perhaps I missed a Year, called it

late at night, "Oh, eighteen, I never
meant it. You weren't the worst,

you could've been the best, if only
I'd told you how I felt, the right time."

Or was it a Decade, the Twenties
had just broken up with my Teens,

and I was ready to swoop in again,
try new hairstyles, consume more drugs,

find pleasure in what I feared was
pain. Damn, I just don't know.

I'd ascend the clock's stairs,
wind her hands to make her talk,

but I'm not sure I want to hear her
speak. I've had nightmares like this:

the mice run, those seconds twitch,
everyone has a knife.

Intercepted by Fire

Our bodies feel light. Strangers fill us
with helium. They really want to see us float
over the city, with its anti-aircraft guns, fighter jets.
Intercepted by fire, punctured, we'll burst in the sky,
rain down on children. They'll stick their tongues
out to catch the bits. We stay under the table,
or wedged in the closet. Our lovers shut windows
so we won't escape. It feels exhilarating to be so close
to exploding. We breathe more deeply, push through
the door. Overhead a plane shoots through dirty,
grey clouds—looking, always looking.

Bears Killing Hunters

Nothing I say has any weight,
one of those particles they've invented,
something that has to be there
for life to work, but hasn't been seen yet.

My girlfriends weren't scientists
so they couldn't hook up high-powered
microscopes to scan my mouth
for signs of sense and intelligibility.

I did try to sign them up for classes,
six hours credit for breaking apart
my sentences, finding a structure
for a void, love inside the wind.
They slept late each school day, asked
me to bring them the notes. Fed up,
I threw away their books, diagrams
of my vocal chords, echo chambers
in my throat they never looked at once.

Although I page through scientific
personals, not one of them is interested
in my field of study. Maybe
I'm a dead science, the astrology
of the twenty-first century. I speak
in constellations: bears killing
hunters, a virgin bringing a dipper
to her mouth, afraid the first drink
might be poison.

Lift your head to the sky:
see, now I'm invisible.

Islands

I

It's always been an island.
Surrounded by sharks,
topped with the hard lid

of a volcano. Sometimes
I think about sacrificing to it,
feeling the body of my victim

twitch in fear. Other times
I consider living here
permanently, building a hut

out of leaves and sticks,
expecting at any moment
for a plane to crash on shore,

its pilot amazed to see anyone
alive. I shall most likely fly
over it in my dreams, a witness

to how small it is, a drop
I can drink from the heavy
glass of the ocean. I choose

this place for my fantasies,
where I had a mansion built
with vaults of gold and seven

tennis courts in a row.
Or I imagine monsters
parading through the water

to the palm trees shivering
in the wind. They wink at me
as they break everything apart,

my fountains cracking open
to blast my face, the roof torn
off in the turmoil, so the creatures

can see all the people scurrying,
fading into holograms
that their claws pass through.

II

We saw the island form, slowly
accumulating mass, bubbling up
from superheated sources. Soon

birds gathered on its platform,
resting there after sea flights.
A seed in a dropping grew

into a palm tree, and a boat
sank nearby, the only survivors
chimps who snapped open cages.

We waited until it realized
its mature form, then we placed
ourselves on its beach. Wearing

a hat and sun-beaten clothes,
we took up the role of stranded
castaways. We spelled HELP!

in the dirt and with sea shells.
None of us believed a rescue
vessel would come, or monkeys

would stop trying to steal food,
fight for dominance. What
we wished for was an experience

the cities could not provide.
We wanted to feel our bones
poking out of our skin, our faces

become drawn and exhausted.
Only then could we discover what
it was like to be human beings

instead of brains attached to screens,
followers of light who could
almost forget there was darkness.

Deer

Deer ate our flowers.
Devoured fruit off trees.
We tried posting a fence.
We sprayed stinky chemicals.

Neither had an effect.
Sunflowers lost their heads.
Pears vanished in the night.
We decided to grow deer.

Watch their antlers lengthen.
Catch a bloom of them
by the house, promise ourselves
we wouldn't pick them at all.

One day by the pond
we see three glowing,
eyes bright, flashy as roses,
the full flowering of our efforts.

Their bodies then moved
into the darkness of pines,
so we couldn't see them,
but we knew they were there.

Spiral

The garden wasn't what we wanted.
Tomatoes climbing up vines we wished
were shortened, so they never got very far
off the ground. Cucumbers snarled in leaves,

curling in unusual shapes we hoped would turn
regular. Even peas bursting with green growth,
so we knew we'd never be able to eat them all.
Instead, we hoped for a civilized plot of earth,

with each vegetable and fruit consigned
to its particular patch of ground. That way
we'd never worry about them reaching
into our dreams, occupying them completely

so our faces grew red with juice, our skulls
became dark-colored pods. Someone
wouldn't come along to consume us, while we
were ripe and couldn't escape from their teeth.

No, we'd have no nightmares, no scarecrow
waving its hands at us, no acre after acre
of land shivering fingers of corn, accusing us
of wrongdoing, allowing hurt to spiral in the world.

Fearsome

I used to be fearsome.
My sharp teeth snagged
meetings with throats,
my claws promised
to rip lovers' organs.

Now, I sleep distantly into the future, where time holds
me in innocence, helpless jaws, pale and pink fingers.
Where I slip on the ice and sprain my left ankle,
where I drench a marital spat with tears down my lips.

Once I could leap
so high no animal
could follow me
into open windows
of beautiful lovelies.

I discuss luck and chance with the powers that be,
and how when my bloodthirsty nature was taken away,
I was given the ability to run, the feeling of fright
I felt through my bones, shaking in their muscles.

You should've seen me
slither like a snake, growl
like a wolf. I was wild, then,
without a hope for heaven,
without a care for my life.

Moon Poem

I cannot get enough of the moon,
how it makes werewolves of us all,
tearing apart new clothes, swearing
this time will be the last with her.

Its light is solid—hold it in your hands.
You can throw it at opposing defenses
in a tight spiral of night. You can
eat it on a deserted island, no others
around to tell you it's not food.

In the evening you can bathe in it,
pour it hot enough so steam rises
from your body when you leave the tub,
the mirror and window full of craters.

When it still exists in the sky
in the morning, I'm glad to say
that I wave at it, thanking it
for being our only hope up there,
close enough that we can visit
if we really try, our sweet sister
who bakes romance and leaves it
on the window sill for us to steal.

I'm happy when it starts to reappear
after disappearing within the month.
Give me a ladder and I'd climb to it.
I'd plant one on its shining face.

The Gingerbread Man

He's always disturbed when he catches us
eating the cookies. He doesn't want to say
anything, so he runs quickly out the door,
scared a dog might eat him, leaving a gap
in his midsection. He'd have to be baked
again, flour and water added, to heal it.
It's his least favorite holiday, where all
he sees are little hims in plastic jars,
all with red gumdrop eyes, inanimate,
ready for consumption. At work he avoids
the parties, where everyone munches desserts,
where he fears to watch his boss crunching
"his legs." At home he can pretend no one
wishes to devour him completely. He decorates
his house with frosting, tells us he's busy
with hauling up candies to the roof. We know
one day he'll drop off the ladder. We'll be there,
gathering shards, sticking them in our mouths.

Dancing with the Snake

After Adam and Eve leave we don formal clothes.
Her, a silver tiara and pink ball gown that clash

with her mottled skin. Me, a tie made of thunder,
jacket puffed with clouds, and suit pants that tunnel

deep inside the world. I bow first on the green meadow,
watch her body slither out of the tree's branches.

She cries at the celestial music I pipe in from above,
while I try to recall steps we used to practice

before she left, and I created all things but people
in my holiest garden. Why did we ever stop? she asks,

and I whisper, Who said we did? After all, I can still touch
the indentations on her scales that used to sprout wings.

If I can remember how she flew above the parting waters,
tears melting into lakes, then I can call back everything.

Bears

We didn't foresee the bear revolution:
picnic baskets thrown through windows,

honey poured over teachers and firemen,
cars and trucks overturned on highways.

We should have shut down circuses,
caged them with tamed ones, put more

than tranquilizers in the rangers' darts.
They stockpiled nuts and berries in caves,

clawed messages in abandoned campsites
in ursine language none of us understood.

From our towers we saw smoke in the forests
where only leaves should've risen and fallen.

Masses of fur and teeth ripped tags, broke
into lodges, dragged a thousand fish on shore.

Some of us survived by climbing trees.
Below, bears tore branches down, one by one.

Refugees who didn't fall to grisly deaths
ate needles and pine cones, drank rain.

Our arms grew stronger, our bones hollow.
We stood at the top, begging to grow wings.

About the Author

Donald Illich's work has appeared in literary journals such as *The Iowa Review*, *LIT*, *Nimrod*, *Passages North*, *Rattle*, *Cream City Review*, *Moon City Review*, and *Sixth Finch*. He has been nominated for the Pushcart Prize and Best of the Net awards, and received a scholarship from the Nebraska Summer Writers Conference. He won honorable mention in the Washington Prize book contest and was a "Discovery"/Boston Review 2008 Poetry Contest semifinalist. Gold Wake Press named his full-length manuscript a finalist during their 2015 open reading. He was a finalist for the Washington Writers Publishing House poetry book contest, also. He self-published a chapbook, *Rocket Children*, in 2012, and published another chapbook in 2016, *The Art of Dissolving* (Finishing Line Press). He is a writer-editor who lives and works in Rockville, Maryland. He has a master's in English from Illinois State University and a bachelor's in journalism from Ohio University.

ABOUT THE WORD WORKS

The Word Works, a nonprofit literary organization, publishes contemporary poetry and presents public programs. Other imprints include the Washington Prize, International Editions, and the The Tenth Gate Prize. A reading period is also held in May.

Monthly, The Word Works offers free literary programs in the Chevy Chase, MD, Café Muse series, and each summer, it holds free poetry programs in Washington, D.C.'s Rock Creek Park. Annually in June, two high school students debut in the Joaquin Miller Poetry Series as winners of the Jacklyn Potter Young Poets Competition. Since 1974, Word Works programs have included: "In the Shadow of the Capitol," a symposium and archival project on the African American intellectual community in segregated Washington, D.C.; the Gunston Arts Center Poetry Series; the Poet Editor panel discussions at The Writer's Center; and Master Class workshops.

As a 501(c)3 organization, The Word Works has received awards from the National Endowment for the Arts, the National Endowment for the Humanities, the D.C. Commission on the Arts & Humanities, the Witter Bynner Foundation, Poets & Writers, The Writer's Center, Bell Atlantic, the David G. Taft Foundation, and others, including many generous private patrons.

The Word Works has established an archive of artistic and administrative materials in the Washington Writing Archive housed in the George Washington University Gelman Library. It is a member of the Council of Literary Magazines and Presses and its books are distributed by Small Press Distribution.

wordworksbooks.org

THE HILARY THAM CAPITAL COLLECTION

Nathalie Anderson, *Stain*

Mel Belin, *Flesh That Was Chrysalis*

Carrie Bennett, *The Land Is a Painted Thing*

Doris Brody, *Judging the Distance*

Sarah Browning, *Whiskey in the Garden of Eden*

Grace Cavalieri, *Pinecrest Rest Haven*

Cheryl Clarke, *By My Precise Haircut*

Christopher Conlon, *Gilbert and Garbo in Love*
    & *Mary Falls: Requiem for Mrs. Surratt*

Donna Denizé, *Broken like Job*

W. Perry Epes, *Nothing Happened*

David Eye, *Seed*

Bernadette Geyer, *The Scabbard of Her Throat*

Barbara G. S. Hagerty, *Twinzilla*

James Hopkins, *Eight Pale Women*

Donald Illich, *Chance Bodies*

Brandon Johnson, *Love's Skin*

Thomas March, *Aftermath*

Marilyn McCabe, *Perpetual Motion*

Judith McCombs, *The Habit of Fire*

James McEwen, *Snake Country*

Miles David Moore, *The Bears of Paris* & *Rollercoaster*

Kathi Morrison-Taylor, *By the Nest*

Tera Vale Ragan, *Reading the Ground*

Michael Shaffner, *The Good Opinion of Squirrels*

Maria Terrone, *The Bodies We Were Loaned*

Hilary Tham, *Bad Names for Women* & *Counting*

Barbara Ungar, *Charlotte Brontë, You Ruined My Life*
    & *Immortal Medusa*

Jonathan Vaile, *Blue Cowboy*

Rosemary Winslow, *Green Bodies*

Michele Wolf, *Immersion*

Joe Zealberg, *Covalence*

THE WASHINGTON PRIZE

THE TENTH GATE PRIZE

Jennifer Barber, *Works on Paper*, 2015
Lisa Lewis, *Taxonomy of the Missing*, 2017
Roger Sedarat, *Haji As Puppet*, 2016
Lisa Sewell, *Impossible Object*, 2014

INTERNATIONAL EDITIONS

Kajal Ahmad (Alana Marie Levinson-LaBrosse, Mewan
    Nahro Said Sofi, and Darya Abdul-Karim Ali Najin,
    with Barbara Goldberg, trans.), *Handful of Salt*
Keyne Cheshire (trans.), *Murder at Jagged Rock: A Tragedy by
    Sophocles*
Jeanette L. Clariond (Curtis Bauer, trans.), *Image of Absence*
Jean Cocteau (Mary-Sherman Willis, trans.), *Grace Notes*
Yoko Danno & James C. Hopkins, *The Blue Door*
Moshe Dor, Barbara Goldberg, Giora Leshem, eds.,
    The Stones Remember: Native Israeli Poets
Moshe Dor (Barbara Goldberg, trans.), *Scorched by the Sun*
Lee Sang (Myong-Hee Kim, trans.), *Crow's Eye View:
    The Infamy of Lee Sang, Korean Poet*
Vladimir Levchev (Henry Taylor, trans.), *Black Book of
    the Endangered Species*

OTHER WORD WORKS BOOKS

Annik Adey-Babinski, *Okay Cool No Smoking Love Pony*
Karren L. Alenier, *Wandering on the Outside*
Karren L. Alenier, ed., *Whose Woods These Are*
Karren L. Alenier & Miles David Moore, eds.,
    Winners: A Retrospective of the Washington Prize
Christopher Bursk, ed., *Cool Fire*
Willa Carroll, *Nerve Chorus*
Grace Cavalieri, *Creature Comforts*
Abby Chew, *A Bear Approaches from the Sky*
Barbara Goldberg, *Berta Broadfoot and Pepin the Short*
Akua Lezli Hope, *Them Gone*
Frannie Lindsay, *If Mercy*
Elaine Magarrell, *The Madness of Chefs*
Marilyn McCabe, *Glass Factory*
JoAnne McFarland, *Identifying the Body*
Kevin McLellan, *Ornitheology*
Leslie McGrath, *Feminists Are Passing from Our Lives*
Ann Pelletier, *Letter That Never*
Ayaz Pirani, *Happy You Are Here*
W.T. Pfefferle, *My Coolest Shirt*
Jacklyn Potter, Dwaine Rieves, Gary Stein, eds.,
    Cabin Fever: Poets at Joaquin Miller's Cabin
Robert Sargent, *Aspects of a Southern Story*
    & A Woman from Memphis
Miles Waggener, *Superstition Freeway*
Fritz Ward, *Tsunami Diorama*
Amber West, *Hen & God*
Nancy White, ed., *Word for Word*

CPSIA information can be obtained
at www.ICGtesting.com
Printed in the USA
FFOW02n2141010518
46435965-48300FF